Books by **Judy Juanita**

FICTION

Virgin Soul

ESSAYS

DeFacto Feminism: Essays Straight Outta Oakland

FOUR GENRE HANDBOOKS

Homage to the Black Arts Movement:
A Handbook

The Black Experience in Four Genres: A Handbook

The Black Experience in Four Genres: A Handbook

Judy Juanita

EquiDistance Press
Oakland, CA

The Black Experience in Four Genres: A Handbook

ISBN-13: 978-0-9716352-0-3

EquiDistance Press
490 Lake Park Avenue`
P.O. Box 16053
Oakland, CA 94610
whoknewyouknew@gmail.com

Acknowledgments: "The Gun as Ultimate Performance Poem" in *The Weeklings*; "Making Room" in *Good News*; "Bling" in *PoetryMonthly.com*. "The Gun as Ultimate Performance Poem" and "Bling" were nominated in 2014 and 2015 for the Pushcart Prize. Thanks to the Rini Templeton Memorial Fund and The California Ethnic and Multicultural Archives, UCSB, for the artwork.

INTRODUCTION

Four pieces in this text by writer Judy Juanita – a poem, drama, short story and essay – bring themes of

- self-determination & ethnic pride
- grief and regret, and
- the gun as romantic symbol or literal destruction

to college, high school and middle school students and to general readers. Questions for classroom or group use follow each piece. Each explores the African-American experience in different eras.

The play is suitable for amateur theater productions or as a film script. The poem can be a monologue suitable for drama, speech, civics class or an audition. The play takes place in the 1950s: a rebellious teen wins an essay contest on Americanism but is angered that her best friend's more militant essay didn't win. Her conservative mother wants her to accept it proudly. The play takes about an hour to stage or read in class, with six main characters and three minor characters.

The poem spans the black experience from slavery to the present in 344 words.

The short story, 1,764 words, involves a woman picturing the child she never had. Abortion, memory, motherhood, and the power of the unknown haunt her.

The essay debates the impact of the 1960s infatuation with the gun and ensuing post – Trayvon Martin disenchantment. The author, a native of Berkeley who lives in Oakland, often uses Oakland and California as a setting.

"Heaven's Hold" was produced at Brava! Theatre, SF., in 1993.

"BLING" and "The Gun as Ultimate Performance Poem" were nominated for Pushcart Prizes after appearing, respectively, in *PoetryMonthly.com* and *TheWeeklings.com*.

"Making Room" was published in *Good News*.

TABLE OF CONTENTS

play or film script

HEAVEN'S HOLD

"Heaven's Hold" is a two-act play about a black teen in Oakland in 1959 who wins an essay contest on "Americanism" and balks at giving a predictable acceptance speech. Her conservative mother has sheltered her after her father's death and struggles to keep a lid on every aspect of her daughter's life.

Characters– requires nine actors (six if double casting of cops and WFL)

Lydja: a 13-year-old black girl, smart, curious and itching to burst out of the cocoon her mother has created around her. She has a burning awareness of black history and racial injustice, partly inherited from her deceased father who was a "race man."

Anna: her mother, a seamstress, widowed, age 34, whose straight-laced demeanor belies a passionate yearning to express herself and give in to worldliness.

Odessa: Anna's aunt, in her late fifties and holding, as salty as they come.

Shad: Anna's brother, 30, a handsome intellectualizing hip cat who hangs with the Beatniks and takes classes all over the Bay Area partly out of interest and partly to meet female conquests.

Ava: Lydja's best girlfriend, 14, unspoiled, from a family of nine children. Though not book smart, she is more developed and street-smart than Lydja.

Thaddeus: their preacher's son

AND

Two cops: (used in a tableau in one scene)

White Face Lady: A black woman of an indeterminate age who wears a white paste on her hands and face, and who wears white/pastel clothes, white stockings and pumps.

Act 1, 8 scenes. Act 2, 9 scenes.

Setting: This drama takes place in Oakland, California, in 1959, on the cusp of the broad social changes of the sixties.

Synopsis: The story unfolds inside the Mason residence where a straight-laced widow, Anna, a dressmaker, lives her life through her precocious rebel of a daughter, Lydja.

In the initial scene, they receive notice of Lydja's winning essay on "Americanism." Anna is overjoyed, but Lydja resents winning. She wrote her own essay and, secretly, a friend's, making the friend's more controversial in hopes of bringing an old rumor of a local lynching into the open. Notwithstanding her audacity, Lydja is frightened by a woman client of Anna's known as The White Face Lady who has smeared white make-up all over her hands and face and doesn't speak. Anna also is courted by her preacher's grown son who has a hopeless crush on her. Anna's nonconformist brother Shad moves in, and Lydja inadvertently sees Anna and Thaddeus being intimate, fueling her rebelliousness. Shad takes Lydja to a college hoop game, but gets busted with weed on him. Lydja begs Anna to bail him out but Anna is disgusted with Shad's freewheeling ways. Lydja goes to the jail to get Shad out but ends up in the woods looking for evidence of the lynching. Shad finds her and explains a different instance of racial injustice. Lydja gives the speech and pleases everyone and herself.

HEAVEN'S HOLD

Act 1, Scene 1

INT. HOUSE – AFTERNOON

(Lydja, Anna)

Anna is checking the shutters. Their living room is part dressmaker's studio. A dressmaker's form, bolts of cloth stand against the wall, and a set of sewing machines, one modern, the other a trundle with foot, fill the room. A clang of the mail slot is heard and magazines, Ebony, Life, and circulars, letters spill onto the space by the door. Lydja walks toward the mail slot.

LYDJA

The mail.

ANNA

Go on, Dear. I've got to close these blinds.

LYDJA

Dear, what if the most important news of your life was waiting? Would you have to shut and close every cabinet?
(Anna keeps closing and shutting)
If this were my house.

ANNA

This is your house. We live here together.

LYDJA

When I grow up, I'm not having curtains.
(She goes over to the window, sweeps the drape open; Anna squints at the sunlight)
And everything's going to be wide open.
(Goes back to the mail)
Too much of anything is not good. I'm quoting you directly.
(Goes through the mail)

ANNA

Is the contest notice there?
(Lydja nods, Anna holds the mail, trembles, clutches it to her chest, closes her eyes, prays)
Oh, God.

LYDJA

You're not praying? Prayer can't change the judges' decision. What could you be praying for?

ANNA

Lydja, I'm so anxious, I can't even bend my fingers. Look.
(Holds fingers out, eyes still closed)

LYDJA

(Holds Anna's fingers, speaks in a spooky voice)
If I win, you have to do anything I say. If I lose –

ANNA

Just open it, Lydja.

LYDJA

(Opens the envelope, reads it silently, looks at her mother's face.)
I guess I won.

ANNA

(Lets out a gasp, takes letter, reads it)
"We are pleased to announce your essay on Americanism has won first prize."
(Lets out a whoop, throws up arms)

LYDJA

Dear, let me see.
(Takes the letter from her mother, reads it carefully)

ANNA

Oh, Jesus. My prayers have been answered. Dear, I'm so proud.

LYDJA

(Not at all happy; holds the letter out)
I bet the teachers' committee never even read Ava's.
(Anna hugs her but she breaks loose from Anna's embrace)
I bet they never even submitted Ava's paper to the finals.

ANNA

Lydja, this is such an honor. Even though I half expected it.

LYDJA

They were prejudiced.

ANNA

Lydja, this is unbecoming. You should not doubt your teachers.

LYDJA

Ava's essay didn't even get honorable mention. They didn't want her essay. It's too controversial.

ANNA

Controversial? Lydja, little boy crazy Ava?

LYDJA

Whenever I say something you don't want to believe, you start the littles. Little boy crazy Ava.

ANNA

(Sits down on the couch, rereads letter)The last time I got a letter like this was back in '55. Shad was admitted to U.C. Berkeley, after he had come back from Korea. My smart brother could have been the first lawyer in the family, the first doctor. Anything. And he chose to fritter it away. On wine, women and bongo playing. (goes to dress form, starts making adjustments with letter tucked under her arm) As God is my witness, it won't happen twice.

LYDJA

Don't you even want to know why Ava's essay should have won?

ANNA

Why is Ava's essay so important to you?

LYDJA

The reason why mine won and hers didn't even stand a chance? She wrote about the boy they lynched in Richmond in 1944.

ANNA

Lydja, that rumor gets kicked around every time a bunch of old folks start drinking.

LYDJA

But if no one ever investigates, we'll never know. Why is one black boy dying in Richmond, California, not important to anyone?

ANNA

(holds up letter)
This is important. I don't see why you're not happy about it.

LYDJA

Her essay was better than the one that won.

ANNA

How could it have been better if Ava wrote it?

LYDJA

Because it was about something. What is Americanism? A catchword. Lynching is a fact. Americanism doesn't take your life.

ANNA

(walks toward kitchen; then turns around)
Your life is headed in one direction, and Ava's in another.

LYDJA

Ava wanted to use her speech to tell about the lynching and our real history.

ANNA

But Ava didn't win. You did.

LYDJA

I don't want to get up and talk about Americanism, like an uncle tom or something.

ANNA

You're going to win a $500 prize and spoil the moment for yourself and the rest of us?

LYDJA

Didn't say what I'm going to do.

ANNA

I don't agree with your ingratitude. Not for a minute.

LYDJA

But you agree with this, 'Dear? "And this above all to thine own self be true. Then, as sure as night follows day, thou canst be false to any man."

ANNA

"Canst not". Goodness, I learned that when I was a girl… It's the Bible, right?

LYDJA

No. But it's right, don't you think?

ANNA

Yes, of course, one has to answer to oneself.

LYDJA

So, 'Dear, I have to answer to myself.

ANNA

And to me. Don't forget you're still my *child*. (Pats her)

Act 1, Scene 2

Kitchen-later

(Anna, Lydja, Odessa)Camera pans past pictures on the high boy of Lydja in pigtails, Anna and Lydja, Odessa. Lydja with half her hair pressed and the other half un-pressed sits near the stove, Odessa is standing over her. Anna is in the front room, sewing.

LYDJA

(holding her ear to keep from getting burned) If you burn my ear, I'm gonna get cash money from you, Odessa.

ODESSA

Stop trying to talk to your mother.

LYDJA

(feels the heat of the iron on her scalp)
Dang. I'm talking to you.

ODESSA

Not in that tone of voice.
(talks to Anna in the l.r.)
Don't you think this gal hair need a trim?

ANNA

Just give it a hard press, Odessa. I'll worry 'bout trimming next time.

LYDJA

Aunt Odessa, you pull at my hair like you're pulling turnips out of your garden.

ODESSA

If it wasn't for me pulling your hair up out of its roots every night and gittin' it in those tight little pigtails, you wouldn't have no hair to be complaining about.

LYDJA

If we let it grow naturally the way it comes out my scalp, then I wouldn't have to go through all this pushing, pulling, and hotcurling it. Maybe it just wants to be kinky all the time.

ODESSA

Your hair don't have no wants 'n wishes. Colored women press their hair. If you died tomorrow, I'd press your hair for your funeral.

ANNA

(Picks up a bolt of cloth, studies it, walks into the kitchen with it)

I do not recall buying this fabric. Lydja, do you know where it came from?

LYDJA

Mr. Gonzalez left it here.

ANNA

I thought I made it clear that I don't want Mr. Gonzales' material anymore.

LYDJA

I told him what you said, and he said since it was the last time, you could have it for free.

ANNA

Oh no, I want this tainted material out of my house.

LYDJA

But, 'Dear, that's what my jacket for the speech is cut from.

ANNA

Not any more.

ODESSA

Now, Annalloyce, you being too superstitious.

ANNA

This is not about superstition.
(pulls a skirt from the top of dress rack)
This skirt got snagged on a fence. The dress with the taffeta bodice – I spilled ink down its front; that seersucker suit I made for you, Odessa? If that wasn't an act of God, the cleaners ruined it. Evil begets evil.

ODESSA

Annalloyce, that man come up from Mexico saved you all kinds of money. You making a mountain out of a molehill. If you stop buying from Mr. Gonzales you just gon' have be like everybody else and pay top dollar.
(Turns back to Lydja) Now, y'all want her to look like a descendant of some bushy haired tribe or what?

LYDJA

Aunt Odessa, that is what I am – and you too – a descendant of a Bush man or woman.
(Anna goes to l.r., picks up pieces of jacket cut out and attached to pattern papers. Snatches it up with disgust).

ODESSA

You ain't gotta own up to it on a stage.

LYDJA

We saw this book on anthropology and I saw an African in it. Look just like you. Had your nose.

ODESSA

Not my nose. This came from an Irishman.

LYDJA

What's so bad about being from Africa?

ODESSA

What's so good about it?

LYDJA

Whether it's good or bad, it is.

ODESSA

I is from Port Arthur, Texas, and that ain't even close to Africa.

(combing and parting and brushing Lydja's hair)

Baby, we ought to take this head of hair to the County Fair and see if we can get a blue ribbon …and you want to be an African!

LYDJA

Don't wanna be. Am.

ODESSA

Well I ain't.

ANNA

I'm afraid to even think where this material came from or was snatched from.

ODESSA

Aunt Dolly would snatch up this good material. And if you don't look like Aunt Dolly right now, Annalloyce. Looking like a turn of the century woman.
(Picks up a pair of scissors and clicks them)

LYDJA

I bet in Aunt Dolly's day there was plenty of this kind of selling across the border, and they didn't get so upset about it.

ODESSA

Long scissors, tall scissors, short scissors, that Texas woman had 'em all! Aunt Dolly was where your mother get her gift. Aunt Dolly would go to town with her needle kit
(she spins around, opens her arms wide, they duck.)
If you was walking down the street and your dress wasn't fitting right, Aunt Dolly stop you on the spot. She'd stop them cow-poking people, them ladies in hoop skirts.

ANNA

Hoop skirts, Odessa?

ODESSA

No matter. She have your dress off and sewn up right in 20 minutes.

LYDJA

I wish we had some pictures of Aunt Dolly walking down that street.

ANNA

They said Aunt Dolly stood on the corner with her cloth just like this.
(demonstrates)

ODESSA

Aunt Dolly *put* herself on that corner. She'd have three or four people's clothes made right offa that corner. And if she didn't finish, she'd talk the people right on to they house and finish it there.

LYDJA

Right there?

ODESSA

Right there on the main street just as big as she wanted. And dare you to git past her.

ANNA

Every time I make some change in my business, you bring up Aunt Dolly, don't you?

ODESSA

Yes, that woman was somepin' else. She did this here stitch. I'll be darned if I can do it. In and out, little teeny stitches, then whoosh. Aunt Dolly was the fastest stitch in town. Aunt Dolly would go out and GIT business. She'nt wait for nobody to come to her.

ANNA

I'm certainly not going out on the street and solicit business like a streetwalker.

ODESSA

Now see, you ought put your precious honesty on the back burner and keep ya business sense up front, Annalloyce. The way she'd get somebody for sure was to look at they body faults – big hips, straight up and down shape – and she'd talk up how they needed this and that. Cut it out 'fore they could say no.

LYDJA

White people too?

ODESSA

Shoot. Aunt Dolly didn't care nothin bout color 'cept if they had green in the pocket. Aunt Dolly's rightcheer, looking at y'all stitching and pinning, looking and approving.

ANNA

Odessa, you raise the dead when you want 'em up, don't you?

ODESSA

You don't think Aunt Dolly is affecting you? You don't think this here man from Mexico helped you break even? You think you just blessed and that's it? You think heaven's got some kind of holt on you and this child and nothing kin ever change it? You oughta be glad this child got some Aunt Dolly in her. Let her wear that jacket she making with her own hands. Hear me?

ANNA

I hear you. She can wear it, but I'm throwing the rest of his piecegoods away.

ODESSA

Go head on. Be human like everybody else and make a mistake.
(turns to Lydja; hands her scissors)
You got to use Aunt Dolly's scissors sometimes to cut your way through life.
(Lydja starts out tentatively, then makes louder and bolder sounds. Lights fade on Odessa and Anna, Lydja can be seen, and the sound of clicking can still be heard.)

Act 1, Scene 3

The living room: Another afternoon

(Anna, Lydja, Ava)

A blond mahogany record player is turned on. Lydja and Ava are playing 45s from a stack. Anna is in the kitchen canning fruit. A glass terrarium full of hundreds of pennies covered by a round slab of wood serves as a seat in the middle of the room. They put on the record "Footstomping" and begin doing the dance that goes with it. Anna comes in.

ANNA

Ava?

AVA

Yes, Mrs. Mason?

ANNA

I'm so sorry you didn't win, but I'm going to take you both out to celebrate the effort you both put into writing the essays.

AVA

Mrs. Mason, you don't have to do that. I'm glad I didn't win.

ANNA

Glad?

AVA

I hate to give speeches in front of a crowd of people.

ANNA

(hugs Ava) You two don't tear down the foundation of the house.
(walks out. A door slams shut. She comes back halfway down the stairs.)

That was a draft. I don't want you to think I'm mad. As long as you're here cutting up where I can see or hear you, I don't mind the noise.
(goes out and closes door)

LYDJA

(stops dancing for a mom1ent)

Wait till you hear her footsteps over there.
(Points to the back of the ceiling)
Come on. Now we can play it.

AVA

(Puts on "Please, Please, Please" by James Brown)

You gotta learn how to slow dance to this record. Make your hand flexible so the boy can move it. Like this. When I went to my first night dance, I was so embarrassed. Jimmy Clark asked me to dance

LYDJA

Jimmy Clark's in high school. He's too old to come to this party.

AVA

Do you want to hear what he told me so somebody won't have to say it to you? "I can tell you've been dancing with the door knob. Loosen your grip."

LYDJA

If the boys know so much, why try to fool them?

AVA

God, you're so hard headed. I just don't want anybody coming up to me saying, "Uh, about your lame friend."

LYDJA

(dances with herself, trips over the pennies) I don't remember the way to do it.

AVA

You never did it to remember. Follow the boy's hand. It's going to be in your back. See? (They start dancing together)

LYDJA

I hope he doesn't have stockings poked up in his chest.

AVA

You can feel them?

LYDJA

They're so pointy. Then the point flattens. Why did you wear them just to come here?

AVA

I wear them all the time.
(The record crescendos. Ava grabs Lydja and they start dancing)
When it gets to this part, the boy's going to get real close and he's going to put his leg between your legs and then you're going to feel his thing. I'm trying to warn you so you won't go like that when it happens.

LYDJA

What if I don't want him to do that?

AVA

Scoot your butt out. But some boys are gonna press your butt back in.

LYDJA

Algebra isn't this hard. How do you know how to do all this?

AVA

My brothers taught me.

LYDJA

You danced with your brothers and felt their thing on your leg?

AVA

Lydja, you're not going to feel it on your leg. You feel it right here.
(pats her own crotch) "Do you grind?" – guys walk up and ask you.
(they go over the step, returning the needle to the groove where the music slows. Anna walks downstairs)

ANNA

Is that a new dance you're teaching each other?
(walks closer to them, listens to the moans on the record, disturbed)
Is that that record with the man moaning and begging and pleading?

LYDJA

M'Dear, don't break it please.

ANNA

I told you I don't want that begging record played in my house.

LYDJA

M'Dear, everybody dances to this record. They play it at parties.

ANNA

I don't care if they play it in church, I won't allow it. I've told you that, Lydja. Why do you want to disobey me?

LYDJA

I don't see why I can't play this record. Is it a sin?

ANNA

I will not have anyone beg that hard for anything in the house where I breathe and sleep.
(Anna goes to the record player, lifts up the needle. The music stops.)

LYDJA

Then I'm begging you, Dear, please don't break it. Can you at least wait till Ava leaves?

ANNA

(smashes the record in half, across her thigh)
If they were in a desert dying of thirst, nobody should have to beg that hard.
(Anna leaves the room)

AVA

That's why I like your mother. She's such a Napoleon.
(Lydja gets down on her knees and starts picking up the pieces of the record.)
Your mother doesn't believe in begging but she knows how to get you on your knees.
(Ava laughs and gets her coat together.)
(takes the terrarium top off)
I'll start counting the pennies if you want.

LYDJA

(Anna comes back and stands in the doorway)
Just go home.

ANNA

Young lady, you do not order anybody to go home. Ava, it's time to go home.

LYDJA

(Ava goes out the front door while Lydja counts pennies.)
How could you do that?

ANNA

Do what?

LYDJA

Break my record in front of my best friend?

ANNA

But you know how I feel about that record.

LYDJA

Didn't Job beg God over and over? Didn't he?

ANNA

You cannot compare a rhythm and blues record to the Bible.

LYDJA

Oh no? I have to ask your permission for the hundred and five pennies to buy the record over and over again.

ANNA

But it's not permission to buy that horrible record. You keep doing that against my wishes.

LYDJA

Then you're just being hypocritical. Because you know I'm going to buy it.

ANNA

Okay, I forbid you to bring that record in this house again.

LYDJA

Are you serious?

ANNA

Of course. I am not a hypocrite.

LYDJA

Okay. I won't buy it again. And we will not let hypocrisy in this house again. That's our covenant. And I'll hold you to it.

Act 1, Scene 4

Characters: Anna, White Face Lady

Setting: Living Room, at dusk

(The White Face Lady has a white floury paste smeared on her hands, forearms, face. She stands on a chair, in her slip, with her bare arms and shoulders, which are NOT white but brown. Anna is fitting her skirt on her, pinning it, for hemming. They talk but only say the word Mrs., each with different tone, then with similiar tone. It is the only word they say but it is conversation for them.)

ANNA

Mrs.?

WFL

(turns to look at herself in the mirror which Anna holds up) Mrs.! (gets down)

ANNA

Mrs.? (holds up a bolt of pastel cloth)

WFL

(approves) Mrs.

ANNA

(twists it around her own waist and does a little dance) Mrs.

WFL

(looks on wistfully and begins to dress) Mrs.

ANNA

(businesslike again, shows WFL a pattern) Mrs.?

WFL

(shakes her head vigorously) Mrs.!

ANNA

(shrugs) Mrs.

WFL

(pulls her wallet out of her purse, pays Anna) Mrs.?

ANNA

(indicates it is too much) Mrs.

WFL

(insists) Mrs.!

ANNA

(insists) Mrs.!

WFL

(puts her money away as if to say, *Okay, don't take my money*) Mrs.!

ANNA

(apologetic) Mrs.

WFL

(gets ready to leave, slips the money onto the table) Mrs.

ANNA

(doesn't see WFL leave money, points to calendar, letting her know her dress will be ready on a certain date) Mrs.

WFL

Mrs. (leaves. Once she's gone, Anna sits down to sew, looking satisfied.)

Act 1, Scene 5

Living Room: The next day.

Lydja, Anna, Shad, Odessa

Lydja is standing on a chair and twirling. Anna is pinning the hem of Lydja's half-made dress, checking it in front of a full-length mirror.

ANNA

You have to be perfectly still. Stop being silly. You can't give a speech and pick up your prize from a hospital bed.

LYDJA

(examines her scalp in the mirror)
Dear, if you make this part in my hair any wider, the people in the audience are gonna think Moses used the top of my head for the Red Sea.

ANNA

Don't blaspheme, Lydja. Now try and say the first part of your speech.

LYDJA

"Ladies and Gentlemen, Mr. Mayor and all the other turnips and rutabagas sitting around here." You would just die if I did that, wouldn't you?

ANNA

You would never.

LYDJA

If I see some turnips and rutabagas I will. And heaven help me if I see a carrot sticking up.

ANNA

I only want to hear a gracious acceptance speech by my 13-year-old daughter on Americanism.

LYDJA

I'm 13 and ¾. Might as well say 14.

(Big commotion at the front door. Shad, holding a conga drum and a set of bongos, comes in. After him comes Odessa, carrying a foil-covered dish)

SHAD

Coming through, me and 'dessaloo. (Sets his drums down, goes back out)

ODESSA

Man, don't call me out my name. Since you grown, I'll let you call me Odessa. I hope somebody wasn't too busy sewing to get a chicken from the butcher's. And I hope somebody else ain't too high and mighty giving a biggety-big speech to wash lettuce leaves. (Walks to the doorway between the living room and kitchen. Lydja gets down and goes to her.)

LYDJA

(kisses her and offers her cheek tentatively)

Don't bite me, Odessa. That's for babies.

ODESSA

I'll bite you and anyone else long as I got teeth.
(checks oven. Shad comes in with an Army-green duffle bag, books)
Man, looks like you moving in.

SHAD

I am.

ODESSA

Who told me?

ANNA

Shad is not moving in. Just keeping some things here until he finds a place.

LYDJA

Shad's coming here to live?

ANNA

Not live, to stay for a while.

ODESSA

(pulls Shad towards kitchen, away from Anna. Lydja tries to hear)

One of them white girls kicked you out? You flunk out of school? You sick?

SHAD

Sis just giving baby bro a little help.

ODESSA

Do great aunts get moving in privilege too?

ANNA

The Lord works in mysterious ways. The roof needs fixing, the gate in back of the house is about to fall apart. And Shad's here.

LYDJA

Uncle Shad'll have it fixed in no time. (takes boxes upstairs)

ODESSA

If he just didn't like them white girls, he coulda been President of the United States.

SHAD

(Shad and Lydja come back down)
Anna, she can't listen to R&B? You two have to come out of the Dark Ages. This prize says it all. If she can win this contest, she should be allowed to listen to rhythm and blues. And in the privacy of her own room.

ANNA

Okay, okay, okay. But your studies come first.
(Lydja hugs her Mother and Shad and then, in an obligatory way, Odessa)

ODESSA

Uh-oh. Man in the house. Things change. Look out.

Act 1, Scene 6

Characters: Odessa, Anna, Ava, Lydja

Scene Setting: L.r. & Kitchen

(Odessa and Anna are washing greens in the kitchen, methodically rinsing the batches, then squashing them into a deep, stainless steel pot)

ODESSA

(Rinsing) Annalloyce, you need another bunch in there.

ANNA

You're right, Odessa. Rinse the rest of those turnips. Mustard and turnip greens. Uh, unh, mmm. Think I should take a bowl over to the Rev.?

ODESSA

This ain't even enough. A pot of greens where I come from means at least four bunches. And watch the water. These here got a lot of rain water in the leaves, Dear. (The front door opens. Lydja is sobbing, holding onto her purse and books which she drops on the floor. Odessa looks round, startled, comes out of the kitchen. Ava enters through front door) What in god's name is going on?

AVA

We saw the white-face lady again.

ANNA

(preoccupied with the greens) Where have you girls been?

AVA

(sheepish) We were at the main library.

ANNA

Downtown?

AVA

Yes, ma'am. We cut gym and study hall.

ODESSA

If these girls ain't the mice to make a wall squeak. Cutting class to go to the liberry.

ANNA

Lydja, what is going on here?

ODESSA

Y'all hopped on the bus and got to the liberry? Wasn't no little boys between them bookshelves, was they?

AVA

When we were through at the library –

ANNA

Through with what?

AVA

With our homework and finished eating our potato chips and cookies.

ODESSA

Y'all really bad.

ANNA

Hmmph

ODESSA

Eating in the liberry…cutting school…unh, unh, unh.

LYDJA

She was right behind me. We were waiting at 14th and Broadway for the light to change.

AVA

It was so spooky. She came right up behind Lydja and Lydja turned around, looking for me.

LYDJA

And she was right in back of me. Like a ghost. Why does she wear that white stuff on her face?

ODESSA

Annalloyce, this child near 'bout hysterical.

LYDJA

Doesn't she know she looks crazy? Crazy. So crazy. And you can see her skin. It's still brown at the edges. And she just stared at me even when I screamed.

ANNA

Lydja, I want you to come in the kitchen. I want you to take aspirin and some water.

LYDJA

I can't, I can't. It'll be worse. I'll have nightmares. You know that, M'Dear. Don't make me.

ODESSA

That child still can't swallow pills?

ANNA

No. But she can chew them. (takes Lydja into the kitchen)

ODESSA

(To Ava) Y'all know that crazy lady is your punishment for skipping school. Two little nappy-headed sugar babies think they so smart don't need to obey. Serves you right... prolly why she so crazy now. Prolly cut school when she was your age to chase after boys.

AVA

(gathers her books up) I'm going now.

ODESSA

(goes to the front door, stands there effectively preventing Ava from leaving) She wasn't always crazy. She was real smart. So smart, she went to the university of Berkeley, and that was a real rarity then, and I heard when she finished she fell in love with some white man – and I tell you, you can trace every trouble in the race to when some fool colored up on their high horse, done trotted over to the other side. Mixing that stuff leads to no good, no good for the body – and when he went on about his business, I can't remember how she fell from God's grace. But she did and that's why she came out of her disgrace covering up herself with that white powder.

AVA

But why does she walk around in front of everybody if she's ashamed?

ODESSA

Oh chile, can't you see? With her face all whitened up, she in the frame of mind that she IS covered up. She might be crazy but she ain't too crazy.(Lydja and Anna enter – the l.r., Lydja calmed down)

ANNA

I'm going to call your mother and tell her you're on your way home, Ava Joan.

AVA

(moving towards the door) Are you going to tell her everything else?

ANNA

No, Ava Marie. Your mother has enough on her mind.

AVA

I promise I won't let myself be talked into doing that again (goes out the door).

ODESSA.

Why you let that child get away with murder, Annalloyce?

ANNA

Odessa, please. She'd get whipped raw if I so much as mentioned what happened.

ODESSA

They have a new baby almost every year. Nobody in their right mind has nine kids in this day and age.

LYDJA

That's their prerogative.

ODESSA

(Turns to Lydja)
You ought to be the one getting a whipping.

LYDJA

We don't believe in corporal punishment.

ODESSA

That's all right. Keep up with these little adventures. You end up like that woman. God don't like ugly.

LYDJA

(Turns to her mother, starts trembling)
God is not a vengeful god.

ANNA

That's not what the Bible says.

LYDJA

(runs up the stairs)
That's not the God I believe in.

ODESSA

(shouts after her) There's only one. And He is vengeful. And you better believe it.

ANNA

(going back to the kitchen)
Odessa, leave her alone. She's been through enough today.

ODESSA

I don't know what's going to happen to that girl. Got too much inside her head. Like a pressure cooker, on the verge of exploding.
Lights fade. End Scene

Act 1, Scene 7

Front door: next afternoon

Shad, Lydja, Anna

SHAD

(It's been raining; Shad & Lydja enter)
Yes, a man can have sex with a woman and not be –

LYDJA

My bangs got wet. Oh no!
(She drops her purse and goes to mirror)

SHAD

– and not be in love

LYDJA

I'm gonna look like a Ubangi.

SHAD

A what? Lydja, this backward way of talking about yourself? Didn't we say hold up on it?

LYDJA

Uncle Shad, if my hair gets frizzy –

SHAD

Nappy, baby, nappy. Frizzy is what happens to dogs and poodles.

LYDJA

If my hair goes back, I have to get it washed and straightened all over again.

SHAD

Are you listening to me, Lydja?

LYDJA

You don't understand, Uncle Shad. You have banana curls, not kinky hair.

(Shad starts scatting)

Make fun if you want. You never answered my question. Do you love Leslie and want to marry her?

SHAD

Why get married and make one woman miserable when I can stay single and make so many of them happy?

(goes to the door to let Anna in; she's carrying bolts of cloth in a shopping bag.)

LYDJA

I'm going to show Uncle Shad the dresses. If he says they're babyish, that's it.
(goes upstairs)

ANNA

Did you take her with you to see Leslie?

SHAD

No, but what if?

ANNA

I don't like it that she has so much contact with my Lydja. I don't like it that she's rich.

SHAD

What's wrong with rich?

ANNA

Shad, are you taking money from her? She's not pretty.

SHAD

I'm taking knowledge from her, intellectual exchange, Sis.

ANNA

I don't want Lydja to see the sordid side of life.

(walks toward kitchen. Lydja comes back down with dresses.)

SHAD

Who picked out these ruffle-and-bow circuses?

LYDJA

I knew it. I knew it. Odessa and 'Dear want me to be a little girl until I grow up.

SHAD

Odessa! Why is she picking your wardrobe? As long as you stay young, she stays young.

LYDJA

Maybe if I take some of the froufrou off.

SHAD

No, these dresses came from a froufrou factory.

ANNA

They're your favorite colors, Dear.

LYDJA

See? They don't care if I look like a baby Huey.

ANNA

What's a baby Huey?

LYDJA

'Dear, it's in the comic books.

SHAD

Not in the good book, Sis, so you wouldn't know it. (Gets coat and goes toward door)

LYDJA

Baby Huey is a big overgrown duck. And I'm going to feel like quacking if I have to wear these dresses.

ANNA

Don't you want to take an umbrella, Shad?

SHAD

(halfway out of the door) Not I. I'm too, too rich with the wonders of nature to hide from her.
(leaves whistling. Anna and Lydja hold the dresses, looking at him. His whistling goes on.)
Gotta run, ladies. Criminology at 4:30.
(kisses them; turns to Lydja) Quack, quack!

LIGHTS FADE. END SCENE

Act 1, Scene 8

Characters: Thaddeus, Anna, White Face Lady

(The White-Face Lady is leaving Anna's; she bumps into Thaddeus who helps her. She recoils, rushes past him. Once he's inside, though, she turns and looks at the two of them, voyeuristically. Anna murmurs his name. WFL walks away)

THADDEUS

You know, I don't scare easily, but that woman gives me the creeps. Got a vase? I brought you some roses. Anna, you're still the only person in the world who calls me Thaddeus with a long a.

ANNA

(Gets a vase from the kitchen) Pink roses, Thaddeus. You remembered Ace used to get me those.

THADDEUS

I remembered. (Puts the roses in the vase) When I talked to Lydja last night, she said today's date was circled on the calendar.

ANNA

It's the date of Ace's death.

THADDEUS

She seemed to be disturbed about it.

ANNA

I want her to remember it. Ace is the only father she'll ever have.

THADDEUS

I hope you're putting much more emphasis on the good memories. (Looks around, goes over to the window, pushes the curtain back to look outside) I mowed that lawn every Saturday morning when I was a boy.

ANNA

And you wouldn't take any money for it either.

THADDEUS

Oh no. Ace Mason was my connection to the real world. He was the most fleshly person I knew. Ace taught me how to drink stout when I was 17, the summer before I went to college.

ANNA

(Looks toward the stairs, then walks to them) When Ace first died, your father-my pastor, Ace's pastor – explained to Lydja that he went to visit the man upstairs. My god, she thought heaven was the attic. I found out she used to sneak up there looking for Ace. One day she asked me if we fed the man upstairs, would he let Ace come back down?

THADDEUS

But he's dead, you're alive, she's alive. I can tell you this much: knowing Ace, if he were alive and you had died, things would be a lot different around here.

ANNA

Meaning what?

THADDEUS

I very much doubt that Ace would have tried to make this house a world unto itself.

ANNA

I beg your pardon

THADDEUS

You work here, you live here…this is a cocoon. It's not healthy.

ANNA

It's the way I make my living.

THADDEUS

Anna, use some judgment. You can't create heaven and earth yourself. You can't keep her in here cloistered away from real life.

ANNA

Lydja goes to church and to school, and other places too. She is active and normal.

THADDEUS

(His tone has changed to a flirtatious and light tone) You've raised her like she was you. Pure, sweet Anna. Do you think Lydja will get married at 17 like you did?

ANNA

(still serious) That's not so wrong, Shad.

THADDEUS

She's different from you. You don't want her to see as far as you can see. She already sees beyond that.

ANNA

We have minor differences, Thaddeus, the kind any mother and daughter have. She likes the doors and the cabinets open. She says, "Dear, it helps me make up my mind." I like them closed.

THADDEUS

As in shut tight, so no fresh air can get in?

ANNA

I want my daughter to be moral and to live her life with God's hand on her shoulder. (she begins to flirt with him back) Surely you don't see anything so wrong with that, Thaddeus?

THADDEUS

I think the church is a hypocrite's paradise.

ANNA

That's not so. You're carrying around your fair share of youthful disillusionment–

THADDEUS

And you're wearing your widow's weeds–

ANNA

Which you will shed as soon as you answer your true calling. Find yourself a pretty little Christian wife…(sits down and muses)

THADDEUS

I doubt if I could ever find a woman as pretty as the Anna I knew when I was a young boy. You know I had a big crush on you? For years.

ANNA

What do you mean, as pretty as I was?

THADDEUS

You're just as pretty now, Anna. But you're untouchable.

ANNA

(moves closer to him, reaches out to his shoulders and steps back as if to disprove him)
I am just as human as anybody else. I try to live God's law not just recite it.

THADDEUS

(he responds to her by kissing her on the mouth. She is surprised but doesn't pull away. They stare at each other then begin talking as if nothing had happened.) Do you think that the church is as close to paradise as a human being can get, Anna?

ANNA

Yes, church brings you that close.

THADDEUS

You can get closer than any church or preacher can bring you.

ANNA

How, Thaddeus? Through sex?

THADDEUS

Yes and no. You can reach God yourself. You can understand the whole mystic experience intuitively.

ANNA

I don't believe that.

THADDEUS

Yes, you do.

ANNA

Don't tell me what I believe.

THADDEUS

I heard you tell Lydja the stories about the little people.

ANNA

I haven't talked those stories since Lydja was a girl.

THADDEUS

Your grandfather was dying and you saw these little aliens marched into the room.

ANNA

Are you making fun of me, Thaddeus? My grandmother who was dying, and they weren't aliens. (goes into kitchen, pours iced tea) Would you like some? (He nods) (brings him tea; begins straightening sewing area) They were feeding my nana a teaspoon at a time, going back and forth. That's all they could get her to take. I had been put to bed in one of those old fashioned beds with the big overhanging headboards. You know the kind?

THADDEUS

How much older than I am do you think you are? Two years, Anna, that's all.

ANNA

I saw these little people, two or three of them, walk by my bed, on the way to my grandmother's bedroom. They weren't flesh and blood, but they were in the shape of human bodies.

THADDEUS

You called them bright shadows.

ANNA

When I told my father what I had seen, he said I had been looking at the light bulb too long. But before I went to sleep, I heard her taking those last breaths. The next morning she had died or so my mother told me.

THADDEUS

That's what I'm talking about, Anna. Your own experiences.

ANNA

I tried to tell people at church about them and they very quickly removed me from my position in Sunday School.

THADDEUS

(starts laughing to her dismay) Anna, if you found yourself worshipping with people who thought so differently, who perceived the Lord in less than that kind of vision, why didn't you go to a different church?

ANNA

I went once, to a Pentecostal church. They were shouting and dancing and playing tambourines and falling out. I worshipped with them in people's homes. And that's where I found out, in order to be admitted, they expect you to have a testimony of seeing things.

THADDEUS

No problem, Anna, you had your little people

ANNA

I should never have told anyone about them, not even Lydja.

THADDEUS

Did you tell the Pentecostals?

ANNA

Yes but when it came time for me to jump and shout, I didn't feel it. I just thought, "This isn't the place for me." I couldn't be false.

THADDEUS

(bends over to kiss her;she turns her cheek to his lip; he kisses her lips anyway, a much longer kiss.) This isn't false.

ANNA

No, it's not but it's wrong just the same.

THADDEUS

You're young yet, Anna. What happens when Lydja grows up?

ANNA

That's a ways off.

THADDEUS

Give it some thought, Anna. Maybe packed-in-a-cocoon comforts you. But Lydja's a butterfly and a butterfly has one task inside the cocoon – to get the hell out.

Act 2, Scene 1

In the living room: Early evening

(Lydja, Shad)

LYDJA

Uncle Shad, do I look old enough.

SHAD

Hey, baby, they don't ask for I.D. at a basketball game.

LYDJA

I'm trying to look like your date or something.

SHAD

I don't take my dates to ball games... You look maybe 17.

LYDJA

That's not good enough. I put on the black tights.

SHAD

The poodle skirt doesn't quite match.

LYDJA

But everybody wears poodle skirts. What am I gonna wear instead?

SHAD

Got a black skirt?

LYDJA

From last year. It's too short now.

SHAD

That's cool. Go black head to toe.

LYDJA

Don't have a black shirt. Have a black vest. That good enough?

SHAD

'S cool.

LYDJA

Uncle Shad, you're not all in black?

SHAD

I'm cool. I don't have to pretend.

LYDJA

(puts on Shad's jacket, imitates him. Joints fall out but she doesn't see them)

I'm cool, I don't have to pretend.
(Sees joints. Feels pocket. Finds more)
Uncle Shad, You don't smoke cigarettes.

SHAD

(picks them up)
Hey baby, these are reefers.

LYDJA

You mean marijuana? Are you an addict, Uncle Shad?

SHAD

What do you think?
(she shrugs)
When you really grow up, I'll let you have one.

LYDJA

I don't want one. Pot is for people who want to throw away their lives in a puff of smoke.

SHAD

Where'd you hear that?

LYDJA

M'Dear. And I read it.
(They get their coats to leave)

SHAD

Don't believe everything you read. Sometimes people who write haven't experienced life.

LYDJA

Is pot "life," Uncle Shad?

Act 2, Scene 2

Setting: the living room.

(Anna and Lydja are opening up the hope chest. It sits beneath bolts of material, which they remove, one by one as they talk until they can open it.)

ANNA

It should be in here.

LYDJA

But isn't the hope chest for the bride? Daddy's medal should be in its own chest.

ANNA

It's in its own chest. Inside the hope chest…be careful where you put that polished cotton, Lydja. I don't want it stained.

LYDJA

Today at the church, while I was practicing my speech, I heard them say something about Daddy.

ANNA

And my laces, Lydja. Don't let them hook on anything, Dear. Who is "they"?

LYDJA

Thaddeus told Rev. Wright that Daddy wasn't a hero.

ANNA

He told you that? (knocks over a bolt onto the floor)

LYDJA

(Picks up the bolt, puts it on the sofa) He told Rev. Wright. But I heard it. He said…it wasn't heroic to save a truck.

ANNA

Lydja, I don't know what you got in the middle of or eavesdropped into but I can assure you with every ounce of my life your father was a hero. (Fumbles with the lock on the chest)

LYDJA

(Sits on the chest preventing Anna from opening it) M'Dear, I didn't mean to upset you. I just want to know what he meant.

ANNA

Don't you remember when we read the obituary, the write-up in the paper? It's all right there, where you're sitting. I've never hidden anything from you, Dear.

LYDJA

Thaddeus made it sound like Daddy was reckless or stupid, not heroic. (Stands as Anna opens chest)

ANNA

That's nonsense. Look, here it is. Ace's purple heart. Hero, hero, that's what a purple heart says. Hero. (She pulls out the medal)

LYDJA

I thought it would have a purple heart in it, not like this…I thought it would be a magenta purple. Or an eggplant purple. Or a grape-juice purple. Not this faded purple, M'Dear. It's like the color isn't even in the purple family. It's just a little used-to-be-purple ribbon.

ANNA

Don't belittle your father's accomplishment.

LYDJA

It looks like somebody pulled all the purple out of it.

ANNA

(Pins it on Lydja) It will look beautiful next to your little bosom in the paper.

LYDJA

(Looking at herself in the mirror with the medal at her chest) It's gonna look dinky. It's gonna make me look dinky.

ANNA

My Dear Lydja, don't be Little Lydja Bitter.

LYDJA

Don't be bitter, be better. I know, I know. I'm not bitter, M'Dear. It's just so tiny. All the men who died for their country, and this is all they got.

ANNA

Many of them didn't get this.

LYDJA

M'Dear, when Daddy got killed, did it happen because he made a stupid mistake?

ANNA

(Purposely ignoring her) Would you like to see my wedding dress? (Pulls it out of the chest)

LYDJA

Dear, this is important, to know the truth.

ANNA

But you already know the truth. Your father, your flesh and blood, died tragically. Accidents are tragic. The brake on the truck slipped and the truck crushed him.

LYDJA

What kind of a truck was it?

ANNA

(Angered, clutches wedding dress) What kind of truck? It was the truck that Ace Mason drove seven days a week to support his family, the truck that bought Ace Mason's wife and daughter this beautiful old house…it was an old government-issue truck, an ugly army-green truck, a dependable old truck that Ace used to carry sugar from Modesto to Vallejo.

LYDJA

But it was also the truck that killed him?

ANNA

Yes, it was the truck that killed him. The brake failed. Do you want to blame the truck? We already did that, that's what the lawsuit was all about.

LYDJA

But Thaddeus said –

ANNA

I won't have another word of "what Thaddeus-said."

LYDJA

'Dear, you can't explain everything away. If I have a question, you can't just 'little-Lydja-me' about it. If my father wasn't a hero, then it's time for me to find that out. I'm big.

ANNA

(Pulls dress up to Lydja's neck. It's too small. She puts it up against Lydja's back) Yes, you are big. I don't know if this will fit you.

LYDJA

At least let me put it on. (She pulls off her top and skirt and Anna begins unzipping the gown.)

ANNA

It could fit. You're almost the size I was. Be still. We don't want to tear it or break the zipper.

LYDJA

M'Dear. I could never wear it. It's faded.

ANNA

I know. But still. (Lydja gets into the dress. She steps away from Anna) I can see you now

LYDJA

You mean you see yourself. (Happy for a moment, Anna hums a few strains of the Wedding March) Was Daddy a bad driver? Had he been drinking?

ANNA

(Twirls Lydja around) No. No.

LYDJA

Then why did Thaddeus say Daddy did something stupid? Why would he say something like that? Thaddeus is not an irresponsible person.

ANNA

(Sighs and sits down) Thaddeus was just a boy then, your age. Children see things distorted, all out of proportion. Come here, baby. (Lydja walks to her, picking up the train)…sometimes Ace did drive too fast. But he did it because he had to. He had to get that sugar from the valley to the refinery and then back to the valley for the next shift. It was the speed that got him from one shift to the next. He worked two, even three shifts at a time…It was inhuman, but he was never reckless. I know he wasn't.

LYDJA

I hate that word "inhuman". There shouldn't even be such a word. …How could he work so hard? I thought bread only cost ten cents a loaf then. Why did he have to work so hard?

ANNA

That was my Ace. Never one to do anything halfway. Whole hog or none.

LYDJA

So even if he did drive too fast...that wouldn't have anything to do with the accident because he wasn't driving. (Starts to get out of dress) I just needed to know. If Daddy wasn't a hero, that wouldn't bother me. I don't need him to be a hero anymore. That's kid stuff.

ANNA

Ace was a hero. Even if he hadn't died, he was a hero.

LYDJA

Why?

ANNA

If the United States government's highest honor isn't good enough for you, I can't explain it. (Picks up the purple hearts, starts to put it away, talks as if to herself) A man pushes and pushes for his family against all odds...

LYDJA

Would it make you happy, M'Dear, if I wore them when the newspaper takes my picture?

ANNA

Yes, Dear, it would.

LYDJA

(Gets out of the wedding dress and into her clothes) I guess it won't kill me. (Hands dress to Anna) I'm too big for this, though.

ANNA

(Folds dress carefully and returns it to the chest) Don't forget the case for the purple hearts, and you might as well take out the letter from the President.

LYDJA

No, M'Dear, the heart is enough.

END SCENE

Act 2, Scene 3

Time: Early evening

setting: Living Room

Characters: Anna, Thaddeus (he is helping tidy up sewing area)

THADDEUS

What do you do with all the scraps?

ANNA

Sometimes I make them into pillows. Once I made a coat.

THADDEUS

(throws a few up; they fall in a heap; he picks up a few, pins them to the wall)) Look. That's in the shape of a country in Africa called Dahomey. If I get in the Peace Corps, that's where I want to go. That could be Italy. (separates the pieces) We have to make room for the Mediterranean Sea. (sorts through) Anna, why don't we just make a whole world of it?

ANNA

You come here to drop off some materials for Lydja. And now you're creating a new world with my materials. Thaddeus.

THADDEUS

I love to hear you say my name.

ANNA

Thaddeus?

THADDEUS

Yeah.

ANNA

It's a nice name.

THADDEUS

So they say. I've been all over and no one's ever said it wasn't a nice name. But no one's ever said it like you.

ANNA

(Shyly, goes to the pieces of material on wall) There's no place like home, wouldn't you agree, Thaddeus? (Silence)

THADDEUS

No, I wouldn't agree. There are many, many places like home. And like is good enough for a place. (He moves away from the wall, she steps back a pace) It's the people at home you miss. (They move closer. He kisses her; she tries to turn away. He waits for her. She turns slowly back to him. They embrace.)

ANNA

I can feel every muscle in your entire body.

THADDEUS

That's a powerful feeling.

ANNA

I haven't been this tempted in a long, long time.

THADDEUS

Why try to break your own record? Let it stand and let it go.

ANNA

(Sighs and kisses him) You taste like temptation.

LIGHTS FADE ON THEM KISSING.

END SCENE

Act 2, Scene 4

Time: Afterschool

Characters: Anna, Lydja (Lydja rushes in the door past Anna, goes to the bathroom, slams the door shut)

ANNA

(shaking the door)
Lydja, honey. Please, baby, what's the matter? Are you sick, baby?

LYDJA

I'm sick? I'm sick? M'Dear, do I sound sick?

ANNA

Baby, tell me what's wrong? (rattling the door)

LYDJA

I saw you…I saw you with Thaddeus this morning.

ANNA

Oh, no…You were in school.

LYDJA

I came home to change my dress. I got paint all over it in Art. I saw you. He was on top of you.

ANNA

Oh, my baby. It wasn't what you thought.

LYDJA

(flushes toilet) It was a man, naked, on top of a woman, naked, and the woman was you. How could you?

ANNA

We... were. You're right but... Will you open this door?

LYDJA

I'm never coming out of here. You were having sex, weren't you?

ANNA

Lydja, sometimes adults have needs.

LYDJA

I love you. I'm the one who tries to please you. I make you happy. I open the windows and let the sunlight come in. Why can't that be enough? How could you turn to Thaddeus, of all people?

ANNA

Lydja, don't make me try to explain what I can't even put into words.

LYDJA

When I failed Chemistry, I couldn't really explain it. But you made me talk about it. How could I talk about the dumb elements and equations and the dumb acid beaker that I spilled all over the dumb sink? But you wanted to hear it. So I want to hear your dumb explanation.

ANNA

I don't have one. I let my loneliness get the best of me. Please baby, open the door.

LYDJA

Don't you think you'll go to hell?

ANNA

If God is a wrathful God, yes. The God I talk to is not. He would laugh and maybe he would say, "Oh, Anna, we all get horny sometimes, even Me."

LYDJA

You never even talk about sex to me. At all. I mean, I come home from school, open the front door, put down my books, go into the kitchen and scarf a whole pear in four minutes flat, faster even than Rayfield Saddler can run the mile, wash my hands after not before. Then I go the bathroom to change my dress and happen on my mother Dear and my Sunday School teacher coiled into a double eight.

ANNA

So you think that I cannot be forgiven?

LYDJA

How do I know? Thaddeus is a bad choice, not your type at all. (Anna pushes the door to no avail, settles for listening through the crack in the door) You weren't making any noise – was it a Kama sutra position or what – no noise, no groan, no grunt (turns and shrieks) My god, did you use protection? That's all we need around here, another body to stitch and cut patterns on, to bring up before the eyes of God Almighty, who, incidentally, sees all, knows all, hears all – even if I couldn't hear a thing.

ANNA

Lydja, your M'Dear is sorry, so sorry.

LYDJA

Then how come you can't say it like this: I'm sorry. Whenever you talk like that – M'Dear would like her baby twickums to go to sweep – you're babying me. I'm not a baby.

ANNA

I know you're not a baby.

LYDJA

I'm almost a woman. I don't need an apology. I need things explained.

ANNA

Thaddeus and I have been talking a lot. About black history. About lynching.

LYDJA

About the lynching? In Richmond? In '44?

ANNA

No, no, in general, Lydja. In general.

LYDJA

So how did you get from lynching in general to naked?

ANNA

I feel like –

LYDJA

Like you lost your virginity all over again. You should put it in a diary.

ANNA

I feel like a –

LYDJA

A motherless child?

ANNA

No, a criminal being interrogated.

LYDJA

But M'Dear, you got caught. Aren't you glad you aren't Catholic, so you don't have to confess?

ANNA

Let's go in the kitchen.

LYDJA

I told you, I'm staying in here for the rest of my life.

ANNA

Don't be silly, Lydja.

LYDJA

(comes out of the door) Don't you know you forfeited your right to ever say that to me again? Ever? Do you know how silly you looked, M'Dear? (they look at each other;Anna draws back)

ANNA

(turns around and starts crying) I'm sorry, my darling child. I'm sorry.

LYDJA

M'Dear, don't cry like that. You never cry like that. (They embrace) I'm sorry too.

LIGHTS fade and a tableau comes into soft focus of Shad,Lydja, two policemen. A U.C. Berkeley box-office can be seen behind the men.

(Shad and two police are arguing. At various points, the roar of a sports-event crowd can be heard, the stampede of feet following a dribbling basketball can be heard. The policemen grab Shad suddenly and Lydja strains to reach him but can't move toward him more than inches at a time. The policemen pummel him lightly, throw him back and forth, enjoying themselves. Shad tries to hold onto his jacket. The marijuana cigarettes fall out. He tries to reach them but can't, just like Lydja had tried to reach him.)

Act 2, Scene 5

Living Room: Later

(Lydja, Anna)

Lydja opens the door, agitated, ABOUT to cry. Anna is measuring a pattern. The material is laid out and Anna methodically fits and pins the pattern pieces

LYDJA

Can't you see anything else but that work?

ANNA

Dear, work is my saving grace.

LYDJA

Shad's been arrested.

ANNA

You didn't have anything to do with it, did you, sweetheart?

LYDJA

Shad had some marijuana cigarettes.

ANNA

I don't think Shad cares if we live or die.

LYDJA

Yes he does. This is his time of need.

ANNA

Shad's time of need. (Anna laughs and concentrates, hums "Lift Every Voice and Sing.")

LYDJA

They handcuffed him.

ANNA

If he loved us, he would not have marijuana around us. You could've been arrested.

LYDJA

We should go see him. Now.

ANNA

I have never once in my life been to a jail.

LYDJA

Maybe this will be the once in your whole lifetime. What are kinfolk for?
(Anna begins ripping out a seam. Lydja goes to the bowl of pennies)
Are you going to judge him, M'Dear, or help him?

ANNA

Let that white girl sully herself and go down to the jail and bail him out. Let her see what loving her intellectual Negro is all about.

LYDJA

(Goes to the phone and dials)
I want the phone number of the Berkeley City jail.
(Writes it down on note pad, dials)
Uncle Shad's gonna need bail. He needs a good –

ANNA

Long look at the inside of a jail.

LYDJA

(Talks on the phone)

Thank you… Yes? I'm almost fifteen… Thank you, sir, for your advice. My uncle is not leading me down a crooked path.
(Hangs up the phone)

Dear, they took him to the county jail.

ANNA

They're not going to hurt him. Jail is for punishment, not torture.

LYDJA

They're holding him until we can post bail.
(Dials again) I'm the relative of Shad –

LYDJA

(Anna has begun to sew, making a deafening noise).
Dear, I can't hear.

ANNA

You need to practice your speech.
(starts sewing again, stops the machine, pins the dress).
Shad has messed up more times than a centipede has legs.

LYDJA

His bail is $250. All we have to pay is $25.

ANNA

Over my dead body.

LYDJA

I can get $25 out of my bank account. I can get it from the pennies.

ANNA

Shad needs to learn the cost of being a fool.

LYDJA

We can't let him sit there and think we're not going to help him.
(She rolls pennies)
I'm going.

ANNA

It's dark out there. Don't leave this house. That is my final word. I'm going to bed.
(Walks upstairs)
What would you like for breakfast, Dear?

LYDJA

Breakfast? Breakfast?

(Counts as furiously as Anna sewed. Puts the rolled money in a bag, puts on her coat, stands at the door for a long moment, then goes and picks up her paper. and begins to read from it as if to Anna.)

"Birdie Eckford was a little girl in Little Rock, Arkansas in 1927, when she and her mother saw a lynch mob dragging the body of a Negro man through the streets of Little Rock. She said, 'We were told to get off the streets. we ran. And by cutting through side streets and alleys, we managed to make it to the home of a friend. But we were close enough to hear the screams of the mob, close enough to smell the sickening odor of burning flesh…they took the pews from Bethel Church to make the fire. They burned the body of this Negro man right at the edge of the Negro business section.'" Prayer isn't enough. We have to act.

(Looks around at the living room, in her pocket, the money, closes the door softly behind her, goes out, where the wind is blowing hard.

Act 2, Scene 6

The woods: later

(Lydja alone, walking from tree to tree, in a futile search. The night noises of the birds, the owls, the wind, crickets, scurrying creatures, resound)

LYDJA

'Go home, little girl, your uncle needs more than what's in your purse.' If Uncle Shad can't go home, I can't. I'll stay here until I find out where the boy was lynched. If I can find the tree, I can probably find a piece of string that was left. Then I'll know for sure that they lynched a boy in '44.

(She falls, gets up, stumbles again. On all fours, she goes through the shrub and bush. She shakes a tree. Leaves fall off; one tree in the light of the moon has some branches shaped like bodies.)

If only trees could talk.

(Walks over to a tree)

Can you tell me where the boy was lynched?

(The night sounds increase. An owl hoots. The trees make a whistling sound as the wind comes through them. Lydia shivers and jumps back shaken. Her purse falls, the pennies scattering. Lydja falls)

Act 2, Scene 7

Living Room: Same Time

Anna, Shad

(The cabinets and windows are shut but the front door is open and swaying. The wind chimes on the porch make a clinking sound. Anna stands still wringing her hands, body motionless. In the twilight, she and the headless mannequin make an odd sight. Anna brings her head to her hands as if to cry. Shad walks in.)

SHAD

Sis, I thought you'd be in church. I guess Leslie put up bail.

ANNA

Shad, you're determined to go down and to take us with you. After you got arrested, Lydja left out of here, saying she was going to bail you out with her pennies.

SHAD

Where's my girl?

ANNA

I forbade her to leave but she left anyway.
(Shad walks over to his conga drums in the middle of the room with his clothing packed on top of the congas. His bongos sit on the floor next to larger set of drums.)

She's gone. And as soon as you pay me back your bail, I'd appreciate it if you would get out too.

SHAD

Hold up, sis. You paid my bail? Thanks, sis.

ANNA

I'm going to keep your drums until you pay us back. Lydja left here last night a child.

SHAD

I have an idea where she might be.

ANNA

You showed her a place she could run away to?
(She goes into the kitchen and grabs a pot and hits a drum in anger.)

SHAD

Get a hold of yourself. I'll find her.
(Shad grabs the bongos and heads out the door)

ANNA

Why can't you straighten up?

Act 2, Scene 8

The Woods

Lydja, Shad

(Lydja has fallen down. Shad walks about, calls her name, beating the bongo. Lydja stirs and rubs her backside.)

LYDJA

Uncle Shad, I hear you. Uncle Shad.
(He gets closer. Plays and sings louder. He finds her, talking deliriously.)
I was on my way to get you out. And Dear wouldn't lift a finger. She just kept on sewing. I have to find some evidence that they lynched the boy in '44 ... And how did you get out of jail, Uncle Shad? I thought they threw away the key.

SHAD

Your mother posted bail.

LYDJA

Dear did that?

SHAD

Blood runs real thick when you get in a jam. Tell me why you came here.

LYDJA

To find the proof that they lynched a boy in '44.

SHAD

(He points to the east.

She looks back towards the trees)

No. You gotta look way over there. The lynching we got proof on is Port Chicago. The arsenal. You might never find out about that boy in Richmond. But we know about 200 blacks at Port Chicago. C'mere. Can you get up to the highest branch of that tree?

LYDJA

Uncle Shad. I'm not a woodpecker. This is as high as I can go. I don't want to fall again.

SHAD

Oh yeah. I forgot. You're a girl.

LYDJA

Forget you.
(She climbs up)

SHAD

Port Chicago is on the southern bank of that body of water up past Vallejo and the Mare Island Shipyard. What you see, if you use some backward looking eyes, is World War II going on: mills, refineries, bomb depots. Men working there, many of them black, loading ammo and bombs from boxcars to ships, mostly white men watching them.

LYDJA

Bombs? Weren't they scared?

SHAD

They're thinking the bombs are defused. It was war. Three squares and a place to sleep. But a bomb goes off. And blows em up.

LYDJA

Oh no.
(Lydja squirms down.)

SHAD

Oh yeah. 200 black guys. Killed instantly. 320 men killed altogether. They tried to blame it on the black men, saying they were stupid and careless when they loaded the bombs. They tried to get the men to go back to work. But fifty of them refused. So they were court-martialed. The NAACP appealed and had their sentences reduced, but they were dishonorably discharged. Some had to go to prison. That's what happened in '44.

Act 2, Scene 9

Some Nights Later

A stage:

Lydja, Anna, Shad, Odessa, Ava,

(Lydja is on stage before an audience, speaking. Her mother, aunt, uncle, and Ava proudly look on.)

LYDJA

…And my hope in accepting this award, which celebrates American values and the patriotic spirit, is to dedicate my energy to the full freedom and emancipation of my race.

ODESSA

(Jumps up and starts clapping)

All right! And she didn't bring up Africa once.

END PLAY

For discussion or writing

1. Which character(s) do you like and why?
2. Which character gets your sympathy? Empathy?
3. What is the theme here? Theme means significance, central idea(s), recurring idea, motif, the main idea that a story is built on, or universal truth of the human heart.
4. How would you stage this versus filming it?

poem

BLING!

somebody jumped off slave ships fr it
somebody else mailed himself in a box
from slavery to freedom fr it
another somebody else ran like hell
from the paddy rollers fr it
somebody stood up to the koo klux fr it
& somebody rioted fr it
somebody sang her heart out fr it
somebody blew somebody's socks off fr it
somebody blew his own brains out fr it
oh yeah, somebody died fr yr bling

even as julian bond wrote *look at that girl shake*
that thing/we can't all be martin luther king
somebody fought just & unjust war fr it
somebody died on parchman farm
at the whipping boss' hand fr it
somebody became baraka ntozake
madhubuti sekou touré so you cd be
    p, snoop, biggie, lil jon, lil kim,
    lil slim, jeezy, uncle kracker
somebody else with perfectly decent anglo-
saxon names~fred hampton and mark clark~
died shot to death at four am fr this thing

somebody upheld our long tradition of thought:
    dudley randall wrote about the melting pot,
    Shove your old pot. You can like it or not,
    I'll be just what I am.
graveyards full of somebody who died-BAM!
BAM! BAM! – not to be called boy

yes ma'am no ma'am BAM! BAM! BAM!
their noble deaths allow you to be "big boi"
somebody bled to learn the alphabet from a to z
    giving you license with all 26 letters
    & the apostrophe

somebody dreamed not this dream
but a way out of nightmare
        & you wake in the middle of it – bling!
        thinking it's free – but things aren't always
        what they seem
somebody died a ludicrous death for ludacris to appear
        a son of emmett and ishmael recklessly
        eyeballing everyone under the sun
somebody's black titties suckled whomever they had to
somebody played maidbutlerdummymammyconvictslave
        so you cd be marilyn monroe in blackface
        so you cd bring hollywood to the hood
        so you cd strike it rich & revere the french riviera

bling bling bling bling bling bling bling bling bling!
somebody gave one insignificant, unsung, whole wondrous
        life   fr it

For discussion or writing

1. Why no capitals except BAM and the title?
2. There's anger, despair and frustration in this poem? Find where and explain how and why.
3. The poet uses many proper nouns, names of historical figures and places. Why? Research some of them.
4. Why aren't the somebodies named?
5. The poet uses repetition. Does she overuse it? If so, why?

short story

MAKING ROOM

When I walked upstairs to my bedroom, I saw a little brown boy – cocoa brown, not much hair, big round baby head – playing in front of my son Khiron's picture. He disappeared as soon as I stepped into the room like he was playing peek-a-boo.

It startled me. I was afraid of seeing "ghosts" or the dead again. I hadn't seen one for a while…pretty much since I saw Dad sitting on the chair in Mom's living room, laughing his head off, his hair black and cut to the curl like when he was on his way to the racetrack. Of course I don't count seeing Riana's mom. I heard her mother died in a hospital in Gainesville on a Thursday, and that Friday I was skimming the freeway to be her friend in her time of need. A lady in a rickety station wagon, with the doors a different color than the car, was driving in front of me. She looked like she had stepped out of the kitchen in her slippers to get some milk. When she got off at my exit, she turned her head – the window was down – ever so slightly and I realized she was Riana's mom. She drove off and vanished over the crest of the hill, into the San Francisco Bay for all I know.

Of course I didn't mention it to Riana. You can't do that. Talk to the relative about seeing the person who just died. People will think you're off in the head and, in addition, be insulted. Anyway, there was the time I told Riana about going out-of-body. About it being a sweltering day and lying on my bed, one minute chilling, the next, a foot above my bed, suspended, begging the spirits to let me down. Which they did after a long while. In clock time it was only a few minutes.

Riana said, according to what she read, out-of-body stuff only happened at death. People don't like to think about the dead or spirits hanging around even though they say Jesus Christ fifty times a day. I stubbed my toe. *Jesus Christ!* Uncle Sam wants another $400 from me. *Jesus Fucking Christ.* Can't you see the no left turn sign, Jeez-us! But I'm people too. Seeing the dead can by trying. Life is very comfortable – at least during the day – without consciously making room for the dead. I'm kind of trying not to get back to the little brown boy because he has a history, a life of his own, if you will. I will get to him because he has to be heard. The dead are persistent.

My mother taught me about the spirits when I was a girl. She said I was the only child of five who listened to her stories. My dad called her a Gracie Allen. Gracie was George Burns' wife and straight man. But my mother never meant to be funny. She got very hurt when people laughed at her and she'd clam up. Whenever she was braiding or pressing my hair though, she told me the stories. Stories about growing up in Oklahoma. About Washington DC where she went after her graduation from college and saw FDR in a parade. About first coming to California and catching the streetcars, and about being the dispatcher in Dad's cab company in Berkeley and the cabbies falling in love with her voice and wanting to take her out until they found out whose wife she was.

She told me about her Papa dying when I was the same age she was then, nine. Papa had caught tuberculosis from walking eight miles in the freezing snow to his laundry job in downtown Muskogee. The family set up his sickbed in the living room so people who had heard he was dying could pay their respects. His last night Grandmother made her go to her room. But my mom said in the middle of the night she woke straight up. She saw these little people, the size of children, rotund and nimble and kind of glowing, walk past her bedstead and down the hall to Papa. When they came back through, they marched back out and Papa was with them. And they walked out but not on the floor, a bit above it.

Of course she doesn't tell this to every Tom, Dick and Harry. My mom's a fifty-years-and-a-gold-watch kind of person. She was one of the first blacks to integrate the civil service once FDR issued Executive Order 8802. She is Missus Solid.

She pays parking tickets as soon as she gets them and she never U-turns in the middle of the street.

But she knows about the dead.

She used to get these federal credit union loans for when Dad had gambled the money into the Bay and somehow, the way she told it, it was always a struggle. Would it be approved? Would they give her enough? Would she get to the union office before it closed? I suppose Mom was hurrying in that gray Ford with as much an eye for the loans as Dad had for his horses – Misty Light, Pretty Patty or Rump the Roast – rounding that last lap at Golden Gate Fields. Dad kidded before he died that the only reason their marriage lasted was because they always had two cars.

On one of her trips to the credit union, she encountered someone walking down the stairs as she was going up, Mom with her worried head down, suppliant, thinking I'm sure of those five open mouths, parted like the beaks of wrens. She said the person bumped into her and smiled and caused her to look up for a minute. But Mom was concentrating on the loan. As soon as they passed one another, Mom realized it was a woman with "great big huge upside-down teeth." She looked back. But the woman was gone.

Of course she got the money, cashed the check, fed us, comforted us to sleep, locked my Dad out of the house for the night and thanked the good Lord for the angel on the stairs who had been there to tell her it was all going to work out.

I still look at people's teeth like I'm going to spot divinity there. *Jesus Christ*. Like divinity is a guessing game. I hope it's not. But you do have to be on your toes to keep up with the dead. The ones I've seen move quickly. And, for some reason, I'm usually tired or stressed when they whiz by. I saw Dad streak by in a car down 69th one day, looking like Joe Louis in his prime. It reminded me of how he and Mom argued over money (do married people argue about anything else?) and he backed out of the driveway at 30 mph. Thank goodness no car was coming. When I dream of Dad, he looks like the Brown Bomber. He and Joe favored even in old age.

Before I tell about the little brown boy, I have to tell my dad's favorite Joe Louis story.

Dad was a Tuskegee Airman, 337th, W.W.II, serving in Italy; Joe Louis back in the states was at his peak as The Brown Bomber. Dad's CO came up with a brilliant idea: get the real Joe and the look-alike Joe in an exhibition bout. Dad went along for a minute. Then, being a bright guy and knowing the real Joe wasn't famous for his smarts, my dad said to himself, what if the real Joe forgets it's a fake fight? Dad bowed out.

The little brown boy playing with Khiron's picture–that's what got me. I keep that picture–one of those 8½ by 11 school photos–next to my bedside. Khiron hates it because it's pre-braces. But I love his all-over-the-place smile; I loved that age, nine or ten, before he stopped asking, "right, Mommy?" like I knew everything,

The year before Khiron was born, I was, as we say, "out there" and had an abortion. Legal and all. But I had a hard time deciding, getting a doctor, the whole bit. It was a second trimester. I guess not quite a partial birth one. But I had to go in the hospital and, in a way, deliver it. They flooded my uterus and basically I guess drowned it. I remember asking the nurse if it was a boy or girl, and she said in a kindly tone that I didn't need to know. What can I say? I tried to abort myself by taking a hundred Carter's little liver pills, contemplated going to Sweden or Mexico (yeah…and my rent was $87 a month), and finally saw a shrink in Berkeley twice who then okayed the procedure. I did it, mourned it, then fell madly in love, married and had Khiron as fast as I could. I picked the name because Chiron is the god of healing. I fell in love with my baby. Adored him. Isn't that what a mother does?

"Welcome to the exquisite pain of parenting an adult," Riana tells me when I complain about Khiron – the loss of contact, the unreturned phone calls, the advice not solicited.

Exquisite pain. Yet here is the little brown boy. Ever since I moved here, I've been buying yin-yangs for kids, friends' kids, anybody's kids. But my friends bring wine or cheese-cake or juicy gossip. I have this picture of brown boys on the wall, playing stickball, going fishing. I cook spaghetti and bean soup – like I used to for Khiron – and throw it away, hoping rats somewhere taste my cooking and rave over it. I have a yellow rubber ducky on the bathtub, a teddy bear and a wicker chair the height of a ruler next to the window. *Jesus*, I chase enough spiders out of this place. I give them a home. Why not the little brown boy? There's even a little ceramic house on top of the bookcase for him to go in at night and rest his bones. I think the little brown boy is begging me to think of him too. Somebody said cats spend three-quarters of their time being cats. That's why they don't pay us much mind. Maybe the dead are like that. High maintenance in their own convoluted way…*little brown boy, I'm sorry you didn't get to be loved and live a life like Khiron*…I mean, who else knows that he was playing with Khiron in the picture? Who else remembers? Who else cares?

For discussion or writing

1. What did you learn from this?
2. What is the theme here? Theme means significance, central idea(s), recurring idea, motif, the main idea that a story is built on, or universal truth of the human heart.
3. Using one of these definitions of theme, respond to the story in a topic sentence, a paragraph or a short essay.

essay

THE GUN AS ULTIMATE PERFORMANCE POEM

George Zimmerman killed Trayvon Martin, was acquitted for it, and has switched from security guard to painter, boxer, butcher, baker, candlestick-maker, whatever he wants. One round, point blank to the chest = a perfect exchange. A young life for his art. The Gun as art and culture.

The Gun as work of art. The Gun as art form and genre. The Gun makes history. The Gun as steel metaphor carrying the human urge to dominate and lay waste to an enemy or perceived threat. Guns as import and export. Hollywood's Gun, its cinematic ordnance, is the United States' international calling card.

The Gun is oh-so-social, as it erases human inequality. Anyone can obtain one and point…shoot…kill. A bullet has no name, face, race, gender or class. The Gun is its microphone, the shooter but the stand for the microphone. The bullet is absolute, life-ending or life-changing, irreversible. The Gun is clean, leaving only smoke and powder in its wake. The Gun is the ultimate performance poem; the message in the poem is the bullet.

As much as I think I'm peaceable, I keep falling in with The Gun.

I moved back to my parents' house in East Oakland in 1990, in the middle of an intense drug war. My childhood home was a stone's throw from the notorious projects where heroin kingpin Felix Mitchell, as head of the 69 Mob, created an industry of drug trafficking as efficient for a decade as Henry Ford's assembly line. Felix the Cat's death in 1986 had left a fierce turf war in its wake. The nightly sequence I heard from my writing desk was spine-chilling: rapid machine gun fire, a car burning rubber as it screeched into the dark, silence for 10–12 minutes, then the ambulance siren. I never heard screams. Why were there no screams?

Without the noble purpose I conceived them to have when I was a young black militant, without art or revolutionary credo, these guns were unbearable microphones for a shattering community. Guns. Guns. Guns. I had liked guns.

Decades earlier, while a college junior, I joined the Black Panther Party in 1967 right when it split from a rival group of black cultural nationalists. Malcolm X's widow, Betty Shabazz, had come to San Francisco that February for a celebration of his life. One group called itself the Black Panther Party of Northern California, the other the Black Panther Party for Self-Defense; each agreed to meet her plane at the San Francisco airport with guns to protect her. One group showed up with loaded guns, the second came unloaded. The second group had no art, no ability to make history, no message. Though the second group was full of poets, writers, intellectuals and bright young minds, the first group prevailed and Huey Newton, Bobby Seale and Eldridge Cleaver joined the pantheon of holders of The Gun. The activists upstaged the artists/intellectuals. I had immense sympathy for the second group but pitied them (Pitied their women more. How much subservience would soothe a wounded ego?).

The Gun was the shatterer of the boundary between the personal and the political. I liked guns. They were talismanic and palm-friendly. I liked being clandestine, carrying that .22 in my clutch purse when I went to work at the post office. The BPP labeled the intellectuals "paper panthers." This conflict between conscience and activism is not new. Stephen Spender, writing about the Oxford intellectuals said "detached intelligence" was a stance that a generation of anti-Fascists in the 1920s and 1930s rejected: "...personal values had to be sacrificed to the public cause. All that mattered was to defeat Fascism....choices had to be decided by the Marxist interpretation of history. Subjective motives did not count."

The split between the two groups of black militants shattered the viability of "detached intelligence" in the San Francisco Bay Area. The BPP cut through the pacifistic and rhetorical gestures and stance of the cultural nationalists with the pragmatism of the bullet. It resolved the issue of activism. How

active should an activist be? Ready to die for the cause. The BPP resurrected the spirit of Nat Turner, Sojourner Truth and Harriet Tubman. The latter told her charges who wanted to return to the plantation once they'd gone underground: If you turn back, I'll shoot you.

The idea of carrying a loaded gun in May, 1967, into the legislative chambers of Sacramento, the dominion of Gov. Ronald Reagan, into the harsh deadly face of mid 20th century racist stolidity, rocked the world. Thirty black men, armed to the teeth and dressed in the signature beret and leather jackets, had the kind of impact that suicide bombers or serial killers have today. Scary.

The Gun is a revolt of the mind, an expulsion of hatred and thus a cleansing agent. Once it is fired, the act done, the two opposites are united forever, the killer and the killed written into history, memorialized or castigated

To shun The Gun is to fear recklessness, to abhor chaos. Yet activists, oft called anarchistic, despise artists who don't overtly join them. Stanley Kunitz contends, "In a revolutionary period the activists are understandably disappointed in artists who do no overtly serve their movement. The Irish fighters for freedom despised (poet William Butler) Yeats for his failure to give them his unqualified support, not realizing that it was he who would immortalize their names and their cause…"

Bertolt Brecht said that a "conversation about trees is almost a crime because it involves keeping silent about so many misdeeds." The Black House in San Francisco flourished for a very short period (not as long as Felix Mitchell's drug empire) in 1966-67. I was there and no one was talking trees. Eldridge Cleaver's book *Soul on Ice* was a bestseller and playwright Marvin X had plays on at SF State and in community theaters. They formed The Black House and opened it up for readings, political education classes, poetry and dance performances, jazz and lectures. In the Fillmore District, the Black House was a seemingly perfect black counterpart for the hippie and drug-oriented Haight-Asbury. But its split was not only political; in retrospect, its air had a chauvinist aura. Women were often ornamental, breeders not warriors, cooks and clericals, servers not speakers, as if there to divert the heavy thinkers from the heavy biz of the day–fighting the man.

Many cultural nationalists–LeRoi Jones (Amiri Baraka), Don Lee (Haki Madhubuti), Sonia Sanchez–were poets, and poets were the shining lights of the Black Arts Movement. Kunitz points out that the writer works alone, unlike other workers, and the poet is even more exceptional: "Among writers the poet is freer than his brothers the novelist and playwright, because his work, unlike theirs, is practically worthless as a commodity. He is less subject than they to the pressure to modify the quality of his work in order to produce an entertainment. Nothing he can do will make his labor profitable. He might as well yield to the beautiful temptation to strive towards the purity of an absolute art."

Thus when we see the Black Arts Movement and its relation to the BPP, the poets and dramatists stand in stark counterpoint. As student activists at SF State, the Black Student Union fought to bring Jones, Lee and Sanchez onto campus. We formed the Black Arts and Culture Troupe and toured community centers throughout the Bay Area with poetry, dance, and agit prop plays. We enacted ideas we were hearing on soapboxes about black power, black consciousness, and black beauty. We staged the conflagrations that were taking place in urban cities. We were empowering ourselves, our communities and getting academic credit. A natural progression was community activism. In 1967, my roommates and I joined the Black Panther Party which we found far more than a linguistic call to arms. It was a family, the place where you get together on holidays, tolerate the bigmouths, take care of each other, and keep it in the family, i.e. the secrets, the dirty laundry, the drunks, the incest, the beatings. Robyn Spencer, who interviewed former Black Panther women in the 1990s for her doctoral research, commented at our final interview that she was frustrated by our overall lack of forthrightness. I reminded her that there is no statute of limitations on murder, not that I knew of any such event.

However, the most important idea from that time, as I told another interviewer, was that we changed the language, the way black people thought and spoke, the way black people thought about how they were spoken about. A major assault on oppression is to assault it linguistically. Pre-Edward Said's *Orientalism*, two black males from the flatlands of Oakland, California, gave a voice to the oppressed using English in a wholly new way. Jean-Paul Sartre said the oppressed gain the use of the oppressor's language. In one instant, *Off the Pig* tossed back all the awful, dehumanizing, negative ways African-Americans had been characterized for two centuries. Baboons, coons, animals. To come up with this one phrase to describe abominable *behavior*, not physicality, was genius.

In *Virgin Soul*, my coming-of-age novel about that time, I handle The Gun often. The narrative would have lost its essence if I hadn't. At one point, protagonist Geniece shows her proper aunt the very first Black Panther Party newspaper. Her aunt recoils at the blood, guts and violence in Emory Douglas' artwork, with its copious use of the steely black metaphor. The Gun was an actual weapon carried and maintained by party members. It was Art. It was Metaphor. It was loaded with meaning and death.

The use of language and ritual had awed me in childhood where I loved communal gatherings, gospel fests, familial and religious celebrations. I'd worked since high school as a journalist but became disgusted with the narrow scope of the field, its all-whiteness, sameness and predictability. Assigned to edit the BPP newspaper, I found myself embedded in the inner workings of the party, typing, retyping, printing words and phrases like *off the pigs. Power to the people. All power to the people. Free Huey.*

My hands shocked me as they lettered and typed these words and the manifestos they formed. The BPP was appropriating the oppressor's language and using it to shatter oppression. This new use of language by the BPP was as powerful as The Gun and even more so because it aroused feeling and changed the terms of discourse between friends, enemies, lovers, generations and cultures. Being an agent of change meant I aroused deep feeling, affected discourse, found the powerful voices that I had heard in childhood, in church, in soul music, in the pulpit–within my own voice. Thus empowered, I began writing poetry, essays, and eventually moved on to drama and fiction, my start as a writer.

Some would whitewash the civil rights movement and Dr. Martin Luther King Jr. into benign icons of a distant era, outsized statues or memories for annual celebration. Some would not see the movements for civil rights and black power nor the varied tactics of the NAACP, SCLC, SNCC, BPP, CORE, the Urban League, and the Nation of Islam as a spectrum of resistance against the racism that determined every facet of American life. The Black Panther Party for Self-Defense was the fist (The Gun, loaded, that is) of the kid (black people) who has been bullied (racism, oppression, legalized discrimination) long enough by the outsized bully on the block (US govt., US Constitution until 1865, opponents of Radical Reconstruction, Jim Crow, KKK, Bull Connor, etc.). Power concedes nothing with a demand, Frederick Douglass said. To demand is not to ask or beseech. That time when the streets were packed with citizens, students, protesters, workers, mothers against the war, unionists was not an acquiescent moment in this country's history. The numerous deaths are memorialized and well-documented. Did the moment peter out? Vanish into thin air? Not quite. The principles spread into society.

From the virgin soil of turbulence came the second wave of feminism and gay rights movements. The disabled emerged from seclusion and institutions to lobby for public access and accommodations. Senior citizens became Gray Panthers. Maria Gillan (a friend and fellow poet) became Maria Mazziotti Gillan, reclaiming her Italian-American roots and triggering the ethnic white literary movement at once. Bilingualism and Ebonics became recognized as essential curricula. *Caucus* as an intransitive verb meant your group agenda had to be strengthened privately and exhaustively to have maximum impact. *Self*-help, *self*-empowerment and *self*-enhancement became ideals because an entire society had watched the 97-pound weakling (black people) go from chump to champ. Black music, musicians and dancers became ambassadors-at-large to American society and the world. Duke Ellington and Count Basie had been there, done that. But the airwaves and new media amplified the beat, the dances, the Soul Train lines, the frizzy hair, the handshakes, the lingo (*bro*), none of which needed The Gun or its bullet because the BPP had handled that task. Our current heated debate about the n-word is permissible because of the BPP and Black Arts and Culture movement. Ishmael Reed, in grand old man fashion, came out with *Writing is Fighting: Thirty-Seven Years of Boxing on Paper* in 1988. The feat of aging gives one that Yeatsian right to write the story.

A few years ago, I woke up surrounded by Guns. Guns. Guns. My boss at the state arts council hosted me at her South Jersey home during my artist-in-residency. We'd had a falling out after her son had been killed in a hunting accident and she'd had three months of disarray and grief. Without money to meet my basic expenses and no checks coming in, my capacity for sympathy plunged. Angry words ensued. Eventually we made up and she invited me to her beautiful, starkly contemporary home nestled in the woods. We drank wine and talked late into the night; I looked through photo albums as she recounted how her grown children had been hunting when one fired the bullet that ricocheted and hit her son. He died in surgery. I went to sleep in the spare bedroom, too tired to take a good look around me. I woke up an hour later and turned on the light. The room was decorated with guns–handguns, rifles and guns with bayonets mounted in wooden and glass cases. I was sleeping in an ordnance. I tried to fall back asleep but couldn't dispel the images. In the moonlight I saw that the sheets on my bed had gun insignias all over them. For a moment, I thought I had gone crazy. Gun sheets? I had to do some serious calming down. The guns on the sheets and the walls were art, fashion and memorabilia.

I liked guns. I like mystery, intrigue, even devilment. My father was an avid reader of westerns, thrillers and detective novels. He had stacks of them next to his side of the bed. My mother had Bibles, loads of them, modern ones, illustrated ones, King James Version. As far as I could tell he never read from her side, and she never read any of his books… complete opposites married for 50 years. There was no gun. My mother said we couldn't even have sharp knives because tempers were too short in our household.

I would like a society without The Gun. Too many short tempers in the world and this society. The BPP had a message that was received. As it deepened its focus in community service, the guns became purely metaphoric and the party split into factions for and against The Gun. Internecine rivalries sprung up. I had moved far away spatially and spiritually.

I don't want gun control. I want police who are unarmed, peace officers. We can't have that unless we do away with guns. Maybe we can have parks where people play with guns the way we play with dinosaurs. That sounds like a shooting range. But it wouldn't be for target practice. It would be for fun. It wouldn't be a rehearsal for cruelty.

When Trayvon Martin was killed by The Gun, my heart ached. Trayvon was at risk because he didn't know how to cower, a posture that my generation destroyed. He didn't turn tail and run – although he might just have been shot in the back; he didn't *yessuh* back stepping. He fought George Zimmerman, toe-to-toe, and Zimmerman fired The Gun, at point blank range, because that was his creative moment. His high art. His historical moment. George Zimmerman united with his opposite Trayvon Martin forever. And the performances continue, in Aurora, Illinois, in Newtown, Connecticut, in schools and theaters and public spaces throughout the country. I liked guns. I hate The Gun.

For discussion or writing

1. Words to look up: ordnance, credo, subservience, stolidity, castigated, abominable, internecine.
2. Note and defend some of the parenthetical inclusions throughout the essay.
3. How do you feel about having a gun? Owning it? Using it? Other people's right to own or use guns?

ABOUT JUDY JUANITA

Judy Juanita's 20 + plays have been produced or staged in theaters and venues in the Bay Area, UC Merced, Southern California and NYC. Her themes are social issues overlaid with absurdity, humor and pathos. In the one-act play, **"A Moment of Silence,"** a distraught nurse whose teenage son has overdosed falls head over heels in love with a duck. Her seventeenth play, **"Theodicy,"** a full-length play about two black men who accidentally fall into the river of death, won first runner-up of 186 plays in the Eileen Heckart 2008 Senior Drama Competition at Ohio State University.

"Counter-Terrorism," a one-act about a homeless truth teller and her bourgeois alter ego, was produced by the Bay Area Playwrights Foundation in 2004, directed by Edris Cooper-Anifowoshe, featuring Catherine Riddley and Jaxy Boyd. It was at The Marsh in 2008 and subsequently at colleges in the Bay Area, UC Merced and LA. **"Life is a Carousel"** – a full-length play about the forgotten founder of Black Studies – has had readers' theater at Beyond Baroque in Venice, CA, the Oakland Public Library and at Brava Theatre in SF. From 2005-2009, Juanita's plays were staged at the Woman's Will Annual 24-Hour Play Festival at The Julia Morgan Theatre and Center for the Arts in Berkeley, including **"The Art of Benevolence," "Samaritan-ism," "The Alphabetologist,"** and **"The History of Sweat."**

She co-wrote **"Knocked Up"** for the SF Mime Troupe about the RU 486 (morning after) pill. A commedia dell'Arte, it was performed from 1993-2005, whenever the RU486 pill was in the news.

Judy Juanita's semi-autobiographical novel, *Virgin Soul*, about a young woman who joins the Black Panther Party (BPP) in the 60s, was published by Viking in 2013.

Novelist Jean Thompson said of *Virgin Soul*:

> Hard to believe it's been almost fifty years since the formation of the Black Panthers. The novel

captures that time's particular combination of violence and possibility, and the urgency of young people who invested everything in the possibility of change, even as grand rhetoric was undercut by very human failings.

Crab Orchard Review's Allison Joseph said Juanita's fiction "should be required reading for anyone studying the vicissitudes of recent American history."

Her collection of essays, *DeFacto Feminism: Essays Straight Outta Oakland* (EquiDistance Press, 2016), examines race, gender, politics, economics and spirituality as experienced by a black activist and self-described "feminist foot soldier." She is a contributing editor for *The Weeklings,* an online journal devoted to essays, where many of the essays appeared. The collection was a distinguished finalist in OSU's 2016 Non/Fiction Collection Prize.

KIRKUS REVIEW of *DeFacto Feminism: Essays Straight Outta Oakland*:

This extraordinary set of autobiographical essays gives insight into a black woman's life in the arts.... In perhaps the most powerful piece in the collection, "The Gun as Ultimate Performance Poem," written after the death of Trayvon Martin, Juanita sensitively discusses the split in the Black Panthers over carrying guns. She liked guns' symbolic associations and even kept one in her purse while working at a post office. But she now recognizes the disastrous consequences of romanticizing a weapon: "It was Art. It was Metaphor. It was loaded with meaning and death....her incisive comments on black life's contradictions make this essay collection a winner.

Born in Berkeley and raised in Oakland, Juanita joined the nation's first Black Student Union at San Francisco State, then the Black Panther Party where she worked on the BPP newspaper and the Breakfast for Children program while finishing her BA at SF State. Five days after graduating, she was appointed to the nation's first black studies program, teaching Black Psychology and Black Journalism. Subsequently, she moved to New Jersey and began writing poetry, plays and fiction. Decades later, she would appreciate that she had participated in four key social movements – the Black Arts Movement where she first performed her poetry with LeRoi Jones in the Black Arts and Culture Troupe; the Black Panther Party where she edited the BPP weekly newspaper; the Black Student movement and SFSU strike where she edited *Black Fire*, the strike journal; and the nation's first Black Studies Department in which she taught black journalism and black psychology.

Her poetry and fiction have appeared in 13th Moon, Painted Bride Quarterly, Lips, Crab Orchard Review, Croton Review, The Female Complaint and Obsidian II; her plays have been produced in Oakland, San Francisco, Berkeley, LA, and NYC. She has been Poet-in-the-Schools in New Jersey, playwright-in-residence in Oakland and Richmond, CA, and taught writing at Montclair State (NJ) and Laney College in Oakland. She was awarded two fellowships from the NJ State Council on the Arts and an M.F.A. in creative writing from SFSU. A proud mother and grandmother, she lives in Oakland.

Erin Merritt in Juanita's Guggenheim application in 2016 wrote:

> I am the founder and former Artistic Director of Woman's Will, the San Francisco Bay Area's all-female Shakespeare company, which also produced an annual evening of short plays written and directed by women, the 24-Hour Play Fest. Ms. Juanita first participated in the event in 2005. We were so impressed by Ms. Juanita's writing, and in particular her range and ability to write moving work under extreme time constraints, that we invited her to participate for an unprecedented five consecutive years (2005-2009). She was a wonderful team-player who never failed to produce something witty and amusing yet pertinent, and her plays were consistent audience favorites….
>
> Even in 2016, women's plays get produced rarely, work by women of color hardly at all, and older women's work almost never. Since 2013, I have served on the Playwrights Foundation's Literary Committee, and in our blind-reading of 500 entries a year for our Bay Area Playwrights Festival, women's writing consistently outperforms the entries written by men. One year five of our six picks were by women, yet less than 20% of the plays produced at regional houses are by women and according to The Guardian, only 12% are by people of color.

I can also attest to Ms. Juanita's value to the community. Her work ethic and attention to detail as well as her writing skills also led me to hire her for a playwriting residency through Woman's Will. In 2008 and 2009, she taught seventh- and eighth-grade English students at an Oakland middle school how to write and stage plays, one an adaptation of a young adult novel and the other a play on a topic of their choosing – children in war. This residency required her to teach to the VAPA standards for Literature and Language Arts as well as Performing Arts for those grade levels in coordination with the classroom teacher, who was to supplement Ms. Juanita's work on the other class days. This effort involved tremendous coordination with the school, the teachers and our directors. Ms. Juanita created lesson plans that taught the students basic monologue writing, poetry styles and finally how to adapt, write and edit dramatic literature. We filmed the final productions and PBS interviewed the students and teachers about the second year play for a special on children writing about war. It was an immensely satisfying experience for all of us, but more importantly, Ms. Juanita imparted her love of language and writing to these students, 96% of whom were non-Caucasian, and 30% of whom were English Language Learners. Her creative visualization sessions and her intensive editing with them helped them to become more fluent communicators in oral, expository and creative expression and also helped them learn why and care how we use language in different ways.

Juanita is a gifted, mature artist whose plays have been featured in venues throughout the country. Her work is relevant and needed.

www.ingramcontent.com/pod-product-compliance
Lightning Source LLC
Chambersburg PA
CBHW071539100726
47908CB00004B/1442

* 9 7 8 0 9 7 1 6 3 5 2 0 3 *